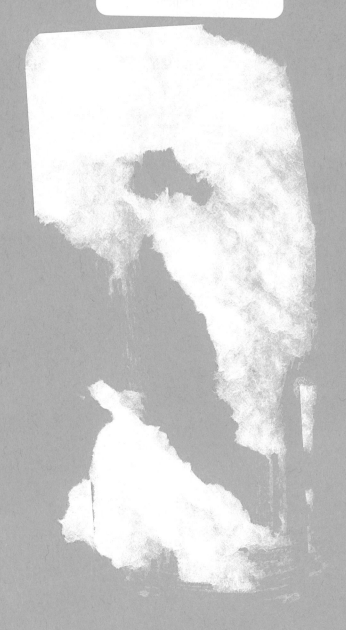

TALKING BONES

Peregrine Falcon pipe from Tremper Mound

TALKING BONES
Secrets of Indian Burial Mounds

by William O. Steele

drawings by Carlos Llerena-Aguirre

Harper & Row, Publishers
New York, Hagerstown, San Francisco, London

TALKING BONES: Secrets of Indian Burial Mounds

FIRST EDITION

Library of Congress Cataloging in Publication Data
Steele, William O   , date
    Talking bones.

    Bibliography: p.
    Includes index.
    SUMMARY: Reveals what is known about four groups of prehistoric Indians from studies of their burial mounds along the Ohio River and its tributaries.
    1. Indians of North America—Antiquities—Juvenile literature.   2. Mounds—United States—Juvenile literature.   3. Indians of North America—Mortuary customs—Juvenile literature.   4. United States—Antiquities—Juvenile literature.   [1. Mounds.   2. Mound builders. 3. Indians of North America—Mortuary customs]
I. Llerena, Carlos Antonio. II. Title.
E77.92.S74 1978   973   76–58687
ISBN 0–06–025768–7
ISBN 0–06–025769–5 lib. bdg.

For those two dandy friends
Dr. Jake
and
Dr. Shelt

Contents

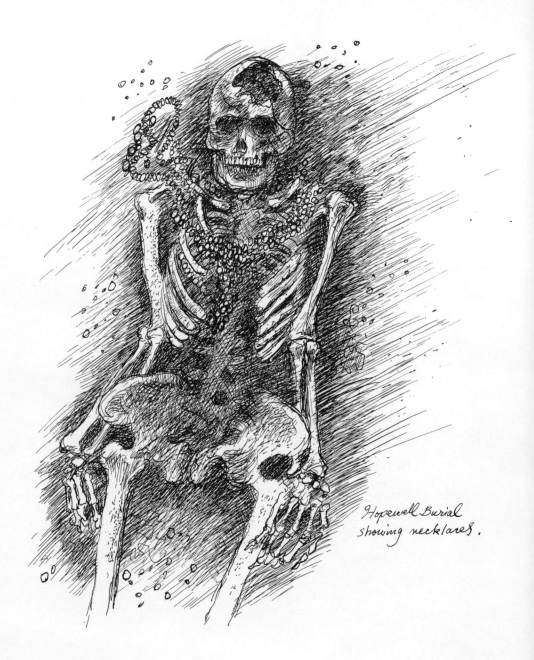

Hopewell Burial
showing necklaces.

I
The Mystery of the Mounds

In Ohio a farmer is plowing his field. His tractor goes back and forth. In the middle of his field is a great mound of earth. It must have been there a long time, for big trees and bushes are growing on it. The farmer has never plowed across the mound. Neither has anyone else. No one knows what is inside this strange hill, but its shape suggests it was made by humans.

There are thousands of such mounds, from the Mississippi River Valley east to the Atlantic, and from Wisconsin south to the Gulf of Mexico.

Most farmers have ignored such mounds on their land. However, one farmer was curious. His name was Thomas Jefferson. He was a plantation owner in Virginia who later became the third president of the United States. Around 1780 he dug into a large mound on a neighbor's farm on the Rivanna River in Albemarle County. He dug carefully and made notes of what he found.

Inside the dirt heap were skeletons of children and grown people. Jefferson had found a graveyard. He did not know why the mound was on his neighbor's field or how long it had been there. But he felt the skeletons he had uncovered were those of Indians.

He had been told by many Indians that such mounds were the burial places of their ancestors. He had been told how the bodies were placed, and he had found the skeletons placed just that way.

Not everyone agreed with Jefferson that the mounds were raised by Indians. These scoffers thought that the earthen mounds were constructed by a mysterious race of mound builders. They believed these mound builders came to America from strange, far-distant lands like Phoenicia, Egypt, Scythia, and the Lost Continent of Atlantis.

The mound builders must have been a different people from the Indians, they said. The mound builders must have possessed building and planning skills. Many white people thought the Indians were only wandering hunters with stone weapons and tools that were inferior to the metal ones used by white men. Such people would not know how to construct the mounds, they believed. Still, no one knew for sure. It was a mystery, and the answer lay within the mounds themselves.

In the early days of the American Republic men often hacked open the mounds with picks and shovels. They did not dig carefully. They often ruined the pots and skeletons and weapons they dug up. These amateur diggers did not solve the mystery of the builders of the mounds. It took trained diggers to do that. These men and women are called archaeologists.

They have been taught the proper way to uncover a mound. However, they know that not all mounds are worth excavating. They do not want to waste time and money on digging into ones which will not yield many artifacts, such as tools and ornaments. To tell which mound they should excavate, they usually use one of two methods. A test pit of any shape and depth is dug. From this they can usually see whether there are bones and tools and ornaments, or log tombs.

Another method of exploring a mound is to dig two trenches at right angles to each other down to the bottom of the mound. Then the archaeologists can see what to expect if they continue to excavate. If they decide to excavate, then the archaeologists decide whether to strip away the earth in six-inch-square blocks or twelve-inch blocks. They will dig with great care to uncover the artifacts layer by layer, as they were first covered up.

There are other methods which may be used. It is up to the archaeologists to decide which method is best. They use shovels and trowels and toothbrushes and even their hands and fingers to remove earth from the bones and tools and weapons in the mounds. They are very careful. They want to see exactly how the mounds were made so many, many years ago. They do not want to damage anything in the graves.

Archaeologists often need help. Though they know how to dig up bones and skulls, they cannot tell much about what these people were like when they were alive. They ask medical specialists.

Jaws and teeth tell these experts if gums had been infected and teeth diseased. The way teeth are worn down helps to tell what kind of food the Indians ate. Arthritis can be detected from fused vertebrae in the spine. Badly formed bones may indicate a poor diet. Thus the medical specialists can learn much about prehistoric Indian life.

This information in turn helps the archaeologist in his detective work. Archaeologists themselves study tools and learn how they were made, and whether they were used to chop meat or crush plant seeds or scrape animal skins. They use new scientific tests to date objects they find—to tell when they were made.

It is slow, hard work to dig into a mound. It took many of these carefully trained diggers a long time to excavate many, many mounds. They agreed with Jefferson that the mounds had been raised by the first Americans—the Indians. The Indians lived in America long before Columbus arrived. It was Columbus who called these people Indians.

The archaeologists learned that different groups of Indians had built different types of mounds over thousands of years. The mystery of the mound builders was solved by these digging detectives we call archaeologists.

Though there are mounds all over the New World, this book tells about certain eastern burials only. The archaeologists described here chose to work along the Ohio River and the rivers that flow into it. And there they discovered the remains of four different groups of Indians who built four different sorts of mounds.

Adena man
1,000 BC.

2
The Adena Indians

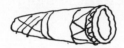

Burial mounds told a great deal about the Indians living long ago, because things they owned and handled daily in their lives were usually buried with them.

Before white men came to America there were no written records. There was no writing on any of the bones or baskets or bowls, so the diggers could not learn anything about the languages of the Indians in different regions of America, or what names they had, or what they called their own groups.

The archaeologists made up names. One type of mound they found was cone shaped. The first studied was on a farm in Ross County, Ohio. The owner called the farm Adena, so the archaeologists who excavated this mound called the people who built it Adena Indians.

Over the years they found many other mounds and

15

village sites in nearby states. They were mostly located in the Ohio River Valley region. If the tools and pots and ornaments in these new mounds resembled those the archaeologists had found in the first mound in Ohio, then those mound builders too were called Adena.

Archaeologists believe the Adena lived as long ago as 800 B.C. and perhaps as late as A.D. 100. No one is certain whether the Adena are ancestors of any of today's Indians. They probably are. Nor is anyone certain why the Adena ceased to be a separate tribe. In all likelihood it was the invasion of Hopewell Indians from Illinois that caused many Adena groups to leave their Ohio homeland and scatter across eastern America. Other Adena stayed to mingle with their new neighbors, it is believed.

Today a great deal is known about the Adena Indians. There is much more we would like to know. We can only guess at what their lives were like by using the objects found in their mounds as clues.

3
The First Burial

This may be how an Adena burial mound was begun with the first death in a new village:

Many hundreds of years ago on the bank of a river in Ohio stood seven round houses of the Adena Indians. Each house had a roof of bark. Children played at the edge of the river. An old man sat smoking in the morning sun. A woman scraped at a deerskin with a piece of flint.

Suddenly a cry pierced the stillness and a woman's voice began to wail sadly. Men hurried from the woods, where they had been setting traps for small animals. Those who had gone from the town to hunt bears and deer returned. Young girls left their half-filled baskets of nuts among the trees and came running. Others rushed from the fields, where they were looking for plants for medicine. Women threw down their hoes and left nearby gardens. The squash and

sunflowers with their delicious oil seeds would have to wait till later for attention.

Everyone ran to the house of the leader. He was dead.

His wife cried and moaned at his side. Then she was quiet.

There was much to do to get the dead man ready for burial. Several of the men took their stone hoes and began to scrape away the grass and weeds in a spot near the town. Then they dug a shallow pit. At the same time boys and girls went to the woods to strip bark from tree trunks, while the women painted the dead man's body with various designs. They used red powder mixed with water. The priest put on his headdress of deer antlers.

He went to the grave and made a fire near it. Indians regarded fire as sacred because it was powerful. It played an important part in the burial ritual. The priest prayed and chanted and threw red paint into the fire. The children arrived with the bark. The men lined the shallow pit with the bark. Then they left. The children listened to the priest sing the death song. They watched his antlers sway as he danced about the fire.

Now two of the men returned, carrying the body of their leader on a stretcher made of poles and deerskins. The women followed, chanting sadly. The men laid the body on top of the bark lining in the pit. The priest sprinkled more red paint over the body.

While he prayed, the leader's wife knelt at the grave. She placed her husband's stone pipe in his hand. It was a straight hollow tube without a bowl. She placed his flint knife with its leaf-shaped blade on the bark beside the body, and also his polished stone ax, so that he could protect himself in the spirit world.

She straightened the copper bead necklace that hung about his neck, and placed baskets of food in the grave. Then she stood to one side with the other women.

The priest threw several more handfuls of red paint into the grave. Then he returned to the fire and chanted sacred words. The women covered the leader with strips of bark. Some men brought small logs from the woods and placed them crosswise over the grave. With one last prayer the people left—except for the priest, who stayed to pray and to chant.

The women went to the river with clay pots. They filled these with sand and gravel and covered the grave.

The men dug up earth nearby with hoes and sharpened sticks and pieces of deer antlers. With shells, children scooped this loose dirt into baskets. They sprinkled the dirt over the grave with care. They prayed that the man would be happy in the spirit world.

Slowly the burial mound grew higher and higher and spread out around the grave. By sundown it was completed. The villagers returned to their houses to eat and to talk about the greatness of the departed leader.

When others in the same village died, they were laid on top of the new mound with the first burial and covered with bark and earth. As more and more bodies were added, the mound grew higher and wider. If a group of Adena stayed in the same place for many years, they would begin a second mound. If they moved to another location, they would build burial mounds there.

Diseases and accidents killed many of the Adena. So did enemy spears and infected wounds. Other Adena simply died of old age.

At last all the Adena culture disappeared for reasons we do not know. But they left behind their burial mounds—some as high as 69 feet and as wide as 295 feet—great monuments to the memory of a long-ago people.

4
The Shell Mound Indians

In some parts of America a kind of shellfish grows in shallow streams. The shellfish are called mussels. Mussels thrive where fast-moving water brings them a constant food supply of very small plants and animals.

For many thousands of years—perhaps as long as 7,000 years—Indians ate the meat of mussels and threw away the shells. Over long periods of time the shells piled higher and higher, rising above the surrounding land.

There were many such shell mounds in Kentucky along the Green River, a tributary of the Ohio. In 1915, archaeologist C. B. Moore decided to investigate them. He went up the Green River in a steamboat. Whenever he spotted a shell mound, the archaeologist took his crew of workers ashore to dig into it.

Indian Knoll man
7,000 b.c.

The bones and tools discovered in the mounds were stored on the boat for further study. Thus the boat furnished transportation, living quarters, and a laboratory. This was an easy and clever way to get from one shell mound to another.

One of the shell mounds which was opened was called Indian Knoll. Moore and his crew removed 298 skeletons and their possessions from the mound in twenty-two days. Moore found these Indians lived a simpler life, with cruder and fewer tools and ornaments, than later Indians such as the Adena. He estimated that these shell mound Indians lived near the end of the Archaic Period, which begins about 8000 B.C. and lasts till close to 1000 B.C.

Moore wrote a report on these Archaic Indians. This report was important because it called attention to the shell mound people of western Kentucky for the first time. Yet it was not a complete report, and much remained unknown about the Indian Knoll inhabitants.

Another archaeologist, William S. Webb, was determined to seek more information in order to truly understand the lives of these shell mound Americans.

But was there anything left to dig up at Indian Knoll? Had the mound been ruined? Webb came to Indian Knoll in 1939 and found a mound five to eight feet high covering several acres. Since C. B. Moore had disturbed only a small portion of the mound in his 1915 dig, Webb decided to excavate more. He brought workers in cars and trucks, not in a steamboat.

Webb and his men marked off the mound in strips ten feet wide. They carefully dug into the mound, one strip at a time. They dug down through the mound to where the Indians had first started piling their empty shells.

They found chopping tools and bone awls used to bore holes in skins and wood. There were flint spear points among the shells, and shell beads, and scrapers to cut fat from animal hides. But there were no clay pots. These Indians did not know how to use clay.

They had no garden hoes like those the Adena used. They did not farm. But they had a variety of tools for butchering animals and for pounding wild plant seeds to soften them so they could be eaten. They were hunters and wild-food gatherers, and shellfish was only one of the many kinds of food they ate.

Webb's group found the skeletons of 880 burials. Some of the bodies had been buried in a sitting position, their arms and legs folded tightly and strapped against the body. Bodies buried lying flat took up more space and made more work. So the Indian Knoll people folded their dead.

Laboratory tests by experts showed that the Indians who had been buried at Indian Knoll ranged in age from three-year-old children to fifty-five-year-old men and women. Very few had lived into their fifties. From the shapes of their bones the experts found that these Indians walked with a stooped, bent-knee gait and squatted with their feet flat on the ground and their haunches resting on their heels.

Dog skeletons were discovered in the mound also. Some of these were tame dogs that had been buried as carefully as the Indians themselves, and a few were even in graves with the humans. Perhaps these dogs had been special pets; some may have been killed to go with their owners into the world beyond death.

But the Indian Knoll people did not always keep dogs as pets. They sometimes ate them for food. We know this because Webb and his crew found dog bones among the bones of deer and other animals the Indians had eaten. Mostly it was to eat the freshwater mussels that these prehistoric Indians came to Indian Knoll in warm seasons.

What began as a garbage dump ended as a burial place, and also as a record of how these people lived. Using the knowledge archaeologists have gained from digging in shell mounds, we can imagine what it might have been like to spend a summer on the bank of a river filled with mussels.

5
The Indian Knoll "Clambake"

A huge mound of mussel shells rose high in the air on the bank of a river. The shells were bleached by the sun. Shelters made of cane and bark and tree branches had been built on top of the mound and surrounding it. These were the summer homes of the shell mound Indians, and they were built to last only a short time.

In fall and winter these Indians lived in caves under rock bluffs far from the river, sheltered from cold winds and rain. Wherever they were, they lived on top of their garbage. Broken tools and weapons lay where they fell under the rock shelter. Animal bones were dropped to the floor after a meal. And scattered about were the ashes from numerous fires. All this trash awaited future scholars for study.

Now it was spring. The weather was warm. It was time for a "clambake." It was time for a feast of river mussels. Men went into the nearby woods with stone axes. They chopped down dead trees and dragged them back to the shell mound. Others dug a hole in the top of the mound with a hoe made of deer antlers. Women and children collected rocks and lined the hole with them. Wood was cut into small pieces and placed in the pit. Twigs and dried grass and leaves were thrown on top of the wood and set afire.

Everyone waded into the river. They all felt around for mussels on the mud bottom and placed them in cane baskets and in deerskin sacks. These they took to the fire pit.

The blaze had died down, but the rocks were red-hot. The mussels were dumped onto the stones. Water was poured over them. Steam hissed upward in clouds. The mussels were covered by green pine branches, which in turn were covered by woven grass mats. The covering of mats and branches kept the steam in the hole. The steam made the two halves of the shells open and it cooked the mussels.

The Indians squatted with their feet flat on the ground and their rears resting on their heels. While the Indians waited for the mussels to be cooked, they joked with each other. Some sang. The children played with the dogs.

Soon the shellfish were ready to eat. The mats and branches were removed and the people snatched up the hot shells. They scooped out the mussel meat and swallowed it. They gave some to the dogs.

In some of the mussels there were pearls, both large and small. They kept these to sew on leather clothes as ornaments. The empty shells were thrown aside to become part of the mound. The Indian Knoll "clambake" was over.

These Indians ate other things besides mussels. They hunted deer and small animals, they caught fish and ate seeds and nuts as well as box turtles and snakes. They had a good and busy life.

When one member of the group died, however, then that person had to be buried. The others dug a large hole in the top of the knoll. Leather thongs were wrapped about the dead person to hold the arms and legs tight against the body with the knees and elbows bent. Archaeologists call this flex burial. "Flex" means "bend." The body would be laid in the grave on its side.

If it was a woman, her tools for treating skins and sewing them were placed beside her in the grave, together with her necklaces and bone hairpins. A man was buried with his weapons and axes and skinning knives. Sometimes trophy skulls—the skulls of enemies killed in a battle—went into the graves with the dead men. Trophy skulls were highly prized as symbols of greatness in battle. Children were buried with rattles made from box-turtle shells and with shell beads and pearls.

There might have been a burial ritual, but we do not know. There are no remains of fire, no lining to the grave, and no red paint sprinkled on the body, as there are in the Adena graves. The bodies were covered with sand and shells, and the Indians returned to their daily tasks.

The shell mound Indians lived a very long time ago, before the Adena people. Their lives were simpler and their burials were simpler.

6
The Bone House People

The Adena mounds are big heaps of earth usually built in low, flat country. They are shaped like anthills. The shell mounds are similar in shape to the earth heaps but they are made of shells, animal bones, and broken tools and other discarded things, and are built on the banks of rivers where mussels are found.

Not all burial mounds are cone shaped or built on low-lying land. In western Tennessee, near the Tennessee River, archaeologists discovered a mound that was oblong in shape and sat grandly on the flat top of a high ridge.

Earth and rocks had been scraped away to make the ridge level and even. The sides of the ridge had been cut into terraces, which looked like huge steps. There were mounds on the terraces, but none were as spectacular as the great mound on the ridge top.

It was hard to build these things with only stone and wooden tools. It took many years of work. Why had these Indians chosen such a lofty site for their mound? What could be inside it?

Archaeologists were curious. The excavation would be difficult, but it would be an exciting adventure too. First they cleared the trees and bushes from the mound and the area around it. Then they began to remove the earth, bit by bit. Slowly they uncovered a house built of saplings. The outside was plastered with clay to make the house weatherproof. Stones had been placed around the outside walls to a height of several feet.

Inside the house were rows of shelves. The shelves contained many cane chests. In the chests were the bones of Indians who had died. They had been cleaned of flesh and then carefully placed in the chests.

The buried building was a bone house, a house of the dead. It had been covered with earth when there was no more room inside for burials. It had been covered so that the bones would not be disturbed by evil spirits or animals. At least, that is what archaeologists believe.

Beside the house was a large area paved with stones that had been brought from the river below and fitted close together. What did this paved area have to do with the bone house? The archaeologists were not sure. They went on digging.

— The Harmon Creek people remembering their dead...

They moved to the valley two hundred feet below the ridge mound, and they uncovered the remains of a large village. Because of its size, the archaeologists guessed it had been the main town of this group of Indians. They also guessed that the bone house on the ridge top was the burial place of the tribal chiefs.

The smaller mounds on the terraces contained bone houses also. They were built with less care, so it was reasonable to assume these were the resting places of minor officials.

The archaeologists knew about other bone houses in western Tennessee built near ancient villages. Like the oblong mound on the ridge, they had been made as long ago as A.D. 1000 by Indians whom archaeologists call Harmon's Creek people, because they had had a village on Harmon's Creek in Tennessee. Archaeologists also call them the bone house Indians.

These Indians were agriculturists; they raised a variety of things, among which were corn, beans, squash, melons, pumpkins, and gourds. They lived many centuries after the Adena had vanished and had no connection with them or with the Hopewell who followed the Adena. Archaeologists call the era when they lived the Late Woodland Period. The Harmon's Creek Indians finally merged with a new population of people that began to spread across the southern states around A.D. 700. Those newcomers are called Mississippians, or temple mound Indians.

Finding the bone houses of the Harmon's Creek people was very thrilling to the archaeologists, because they knew about Indians who used bone houses in the eighteenth century. The Indians were the Choctaw and they had lived in Mississippi.

Travelers had seen and described the burial customs of the Choctaw. Archaeologists do not believe the Harmon's Creek Indians were the ancestors of the Choctaw. Still, they have carefully studied what was written about Choctaw burials. They believe it has helped them understand better the ways of the prehistoric Harmon's Creek people. They think those older Indians must have done things in the same way and for the same reason that these new Indians, the Choctaw, did.

7

The Bone Pickers

If the burial customs of the Harmon's Creek people were truly like those of the Choctaw, this is what might have happened:

It was autumn. Along the river the trees were red and yellow and orange. Bears hunted for persimmons among the trees. Deer browsed on acorns. Geese flew overhead in great V-shaped formations. The days were bright and warm.

The Harmon's Creek Indians hunted and fished. They harvested crops from garden and field. They stored plant seeds and nuts for the winter. It was a good time of the year and people went about their work.

But a great warrior had died and his family was sorrowfully preparing for his funeral. The sons and brothers of the warrior built a platform on wooden

38

posts. They laid the body on the platform and covered it with deer skins.

Beside the corpse the women placed food and drink, a pair of moccasins, and the warrior's weapons. The Harmon's Creek Indians believed these things would be useful to the warrior's spirit in the afterlife. A wall of poles was set up around the platform. Every morning the women of the family walked around the wall of poles weeping and moaning. At night the men came to mourn. The corpse stayed on the platform until the flesh became soft and decayed.

Then the bone picker was called. There was one in each clan or large family group. Bone pickers were old men. They were tattooed with special designs, and the fingernails of their thumbs and first two fingers were long as bird talons. Bone pickers from the various groups lived on the high ridge near the Great Bone House.

The bone picker marched down the sloping earth ramp which went from the ridge top to the valley. He came to the enclosure where the warrior lay, and climbed onto the platform. With his long nails he carefully scraped all the flesh from the skeleton, placing the clean white bones inside a cane chest. Then he set fire to the platform and the wall. The warrior's flesh had been left on the platform to be destroyed by the flames.

Bone picker shaman
at a cremation ritual.

Now the bone picker carried the chest up the ramp to the Great Bone House atop the ridge and placed it on a shelf inside beside other long-dead warriors. This bone house was very special. Only the bones of chieftains and great warriors were there.

At night a funeral feast was held in the town. The family and the friends of the dead warrior were there to honor him. The bone picker was probably in charge. Before the food was served, the bone picker asked the headmen of the various clans to speak. These speeches were long and told of the courage of the clans and of the greatness of their tribe. A member of the dead warrior's family spoke of his life with praise and pride. Then the bone picker called for the food to be served.

There was corn, kidney beans, and squash to go with the barbecued turkeys and venison, fish baked in ashes, and persimmon bread. Musicians were summoned by the bone picker, and a dance followed. This lasted until daylight. There was a final short speech by the headman of the town and the people returned to their huts, satisfied they had done all they could with the proper ceremonies to send the warrior's spirit to the afterworld in comfort and safety.

That was the end of the warrior's funeral. But it was not the end of the rites for all the dead. Each spring and fall the people of the town would gather around an upright pole on the ridge top. This was the cry pole. The bone pickers of the various clans would bring out all the chests from the bone house and set them around the cry pole. The mourners would cry and tear at their hair. The spirits of the dead came close and listened. They knew they were not forgotten. They knew the living loved and missed them still.

The wailing went on for two days and nights. On the third day the chests would be put back inside the Great Bone House and the cry pole taken down. The Harmon's Creek people returned to their town at the bottom of the ridge. Twice a year they remembered their dead in this way.

But after a few centuries another people conquered the Harmon's Creek Indians. Their houses were abandoned, and there were no more bone pickers or cry poles.

8
The Hopewell Indians

In Ross County, Ohio, far to the north of where the Harmon's Creek Indians lived but near the Adena sites, Captain M. C. Hopewell owned a farm with thirty earthen mounds on it. When the archaeologist Warren K. Moorhead opened these mounds in 1893, he was amazed at what he found inside along with the skeletons of the Indians.

He found conch shells from the Atlantic coast, and sharks' teeth and the shells of sea tortoises. He found the teeth of grizzly bears from the Rocky Mountains, and mica dug from the mountains of North Carolina. There was a kind of volcanic stone called obsidian, which is found only in the southern part of the Rocky Mountains and in Central America.

All these materials had been fashioned into ornaments and decorations by Indians whom archaeologists call the Hopewell Indians. There were also

Hopewell man 500 B.C.

pearl necklaces, bear-jaw pendants, copper breast-plates, and ear ornaments of clay worn both by men and women. Shirts and armbands and skirts of deer-skin were made more attractive with designs of mica and pearls sewn on them. All these artifacts were more elaborate and beautiful than any others the archaeologists have found in mounds in the eastern United States.

On opening a Hopewell grave, archaeologists could tell if the dead person was prominent or of high rank in his or her town by the wealth of trade goods—obsidian, mica, copper, and ornamental articles from distant regions. American Indians in pre-historic times did a great deal of trading across the North American continent, but archaeologists are not sure how they did it.

Were the pieces of obsidian handed from tribe to tribe until they had traveled from Central America to the Hopewell Indians in Ohio? Or did the Hopewell Indians send some members of their people to Mexico to get obsidian, as well as to other places to get shells and river pearls and shiny stones? Or did some Indians from the coast of New Jersey journey to Ohio to bring shells from their shores to swap for the things which the Hopewell people made?

The only thing the archaeologists know for certain is that the Indians carried the wares themselves. They carried them in packs on their backs or in canoes and dugouts. They had no horses or other pack animals. When the traders reached the Hope-well towns, the materials they brought were passed to the skilled craftsmen.

Blocks of cataline and soapstone went to the pipe makers. These artisans produced very handsome and well-carved pipes. They shaped the bowls and stems from the rough blocks of stone by pecking with very hard stone hammers and by cutting with stone saws. With flint knives and long tapering drills they carved the bowls. A hole was then bored through the stone stem to the bowl. Later a hollow cane would be inserted into the hole in the stem as a mouthpiece.

Now came the delicate work of carving a figure on the bowl or stem of the pipe. The figure always faced the smoker. It might be a frog, an owl, a turtle, a bird, or a human face. When the carving was completed, the pipe was polished with sand and water and finished to a shiny smoothness with a piece of soft deerskin. It had taken much hard work and many weeks. The result was a work of art and an object of beauty to be valued by its owner in his lifetime and put in the grave when he died.

The lumps of copper brought by traders from the mines in the Lake Superior region were pounded into thin sheets by the coppersmiths. These sheets were wrapped around carved wooden objects such as deer horns or mushrooms, or made into death masks and breastplates. Squares, swastikas, or sun symbols, and figures of snakes were cut from the sheets for ornaments. Strips of copper became beads and bracelets and rings and ear spools. The Hopewell had many uses for the soft copper.

Besides metal and stone, the Hopewell craftsmen worked in wood, carving cups and bowls and masks. They made pendants from shells and mantles from bird feathers. Pots and bowls and pans were also molded from clay, as were doll-sized figures showing the hairstyles and clothing of the Hopewell people.

There were also skilled workers who wove plant fibers and grasses into cloth on which designs were painted.

The farmers should not be forgotten. Theirs was a skill too, a very necessary one. They must know when the spring floods were over so corn, beans, and squash could safely be planted in the bottomlands along the rivers. Hunters too were vital to the food supply that kept the craftsmen and town and farm workers alive and efficient.

It is amazing that this complex system of work and trade and crafts existed almost entirely to produce ceremonial objects for grave offerings. Had the dead ever been so honored?

The great number and splendor of the treasures in Hopewell burial mounds make the grave offerings of the Adena seem humble and sparse. They make those of the shell mound Indians and others seem very crude.

9
The Cult of the Dead

The Hopewell people had the most elaborate burial customs of any Indians of the eastern United States. Later Indians of the Temple Mound Period would erect huge ceremonial mounds and bury their dead in smaller mounds and in cemeteries. They sent their dead to the spirit world with handsome and finely made artifacts. Yet their grave offerings are not nearly as numerous as those of the Hopewell Indians.

Archaeologists believe it was only the priests, the chiefs, and perhaps the most skilled of the craftsmen who were laid to rest with treasures. Archaeologists have found that three fourths of the Hopewell dead were cremated and the ashes placed in special houses without artifacts. Were these the less distinguished of the Hopewell people? No one knows, but it seems a logical guess.

Hopewell Burial

The welfare of the spirits of the dead leaders was the major concern of all the Hopewells. It governed the daily lives of all. It is this cult of the dead, as it is called by archaeologists, which fills the burial mounds with such a wealth of grave goods.

When a chief was buried, he was laid flat on a raised clay platform inside a charnal house, or house of the dead. A low log wall was built around the body. Baskets of pearls and shell beads were poured into the log grave. Birds and animals were cut from sheets of mica and copper and sewn to his garments. Strings of copper beads and bear teeth were placed about his neck. On his head was a crest of copper antlers interlaced with colored bird feathers and stone beads. Copper spools went into his pierced earlobes, and a huge nose shaped from strips of copper was set on his face. Inside the log wall mourners placed many finely carved stone pipes and conch shells engraved with figures of fish and snakes and birds.

Tools and weapons were arranged about the chief. Sometimes these tools and ornaments were broken, or had holes made in them. Since tools and ornaments could not physically be taken into the spirit world, they were "killed" by being smashed or damaged. This released the spirits of the objects so they could travel with the dead chief and be a help to him in his new ghost life.

Powdery red paint was sprinkled over the body. Then the log tomb was covered with tree bark. The body lay in state for a long time. Finally earth was piled over the tomb.

When a charnal house became filled with earthen mounds, it was burned and earth was piled over all the burials, forming one large mound. Another charnal house would then be erected at another location.

From the immense quantity of the finely made belongings buried in the log tombs, archaeologists learned much about the Hopewell. They discovered their continent-wide trade routes, the many skills of their craftsmen, their religious fascination with death, and their appreciation of beautiful objects made from exotic materials.

But the grave furnishings do not tell what happened to the Hopewell nor why they ceased to make fine artifacts around A.D. 550 and no longer cared to place burial objects in their log tombs as they had formerly. It is another mystery the archaeologists have been unable to solve. But they can speculate, as long as they tell us they are guessing.

Some have guessed that the trade network failed to keep supplying the Hopewell craftsmen with raw materials. Without trade goods the artists and craftsmen had little to work with. They could not provide fine articles to go into the graves. The power of the chieftains and the priests was badly damaged by this lack of beautiful ornaments.

Some archaeologists have speculated that the corn crop failed and the resulting famine destroyed the Hopewell.

Still another guess is that a warring group of Indians came into Hopewell territory and conquered them. There is evidence that some Hopewell villages built protective palisades around their towns. Had the Hopewell lived an easy and soft life too long to fight off intruding warriors?

Perhaps someday we will know why the Hopewell and their way of life vanished after five centuries of splendor and greatness.

alligator effigy pipe. Esch Mound.
Hopewell Culture

Afterword

Almost three hundred years went by after Columbus landed on the shores of the New World before white men became interested in learning about the natives of America.

Historians, linguists, biologists, and other scientists have studied the customs and foods and languages and tools of living Indians, and learned as much as they could.

And the archaeologists have kept busy with shovels and trowels, toothbrushes and backhoes, to make the earth give up its secrets so that a picture of the past will be clear and no mysteries remain. The archaeologists who have taught us the most about Indians are those who have uncovered Indian graves.

Those Indians who took the time and trouble to build mounds for their dead have left the clearest records for us. Mound builders usually had great respect for those of their members who had gone before them into the spirit world. They cared for the very bones of their fellow men and women. Now these bones talk to us, to tell us of the way the people lived and worshipped in the years before the white man came.

adena Duck effigy pipe

Selected Bibliography

Brennan, Louis A. *No Stone Unturned: An Almanac of North American Prehistory*. New York: Random House, Inc., 1959. For the general reader, with some material on Adena and Hopewell. A helpful bibliography.

———. *American Dawn: A New Model of American Prehistory*. New York: The Macmillan Company, 1970. Wide-ranging prehistory but a bit on Adena and Hopewell. An index and a bibliography.

Ceram, C. W. *The First Americans: A Story of North American Archaeology*. New York: Harcourt Brace Jovanovich, Inc., 1971. For the general reader. Origins and early history of American Indians.

Dragoo, Don W. *Mounds for the Dead: An Analysis of the Adena Culture*. Pittsburgh: Carnegie Museum Annals, 1963. Technical. Maps, drawings, illustrations.

Fundaburk, Emma Lila, and Foreman, Mary Douglass, eds. *Sun Circles and Human Hands: The Southeastern Indians, Art and Industries*. Luverne, Ala.: Emma Lila Fundaburk, Publisher. Very little about the northern burial mounds. It is a picture book with enough text to annotate the plates of artifacts and help the amateur identify them.

Griffin, James B., ed. *Archeology of Eastern United States.* Chicago: The University of Chicago Press, 1952. Though dated, it is still a good summary of excavations of important archaeology sites. Technical, great illustrations, no index.

Holmes, William H. *Handbook of Aboriginal American Antiquities: The Lithic Industries.* Nashville: Blue & Gray Press, Inc. (1972 reprint). Tells where the prehistoric Indians found the stones they used and how they shaped them for their various needs. For everyone.

Lewis, Thomas M., and Kneberg, Madeline. *Tribes That Slumber: Indians of the Tennessee Region.* Knoxville: University of Tennessee Press, 1958. Authoritative and very readable. A few pages are devoted to Harmon's Creek Indians.

Martin, Paul S., Quimby, George I., and Collier, Donald. *Indians Before Columbus: Twenty Thousand Years of North American History Revealed by Archaeology.* Chicago: The University of Chicago Press, 1947. Written for the interested layman and student of anthropology. Old but usable.

Silverberg, Robert. *Mound Builders of Ancient America: The Archaeology of a Myth.* Greenwich, Conn.: New York Graphic Society, Ltd., 1968. An entertaining and detailed survey of Indians who constructed mounds and the legends these monuments begat in our ancestors.

Webb, William S. *Indian Knoll.* Knoxville: University of Tennessee Press, 1974. New edition of Webb's 1946 publication. A classic work. Technical.

Webb, William S., and Snow, Charles E. *The Adena People.*

Reports in Anthropology, Vol. 6. Lexington: University of Kentucky, 1945 (reprint Knoxville: University of Tennessee, 1974). A classic work. Technical.

Webb, William S., and Baby, Raymond S. *The Adena People,* No. 2. Columbus: Ohio Historical Society, 1957. A supplement to the preceding volume. Technical.

Willey, Gordon R. *An Introduction to American Archaeology.* Volume 1: *North and Middle America.* Englewood Cliffs, N.J.: Prentice-Hall, Inc., 1966. A well-researched textbook with a summary and pictures about the Adena and Hopewell Indians.

Chronology

Cultural Traditions	Major Periods	Dates	Kentucky	Ohio	Tennessee
Mississippian	Temple Mound I	A.D. 700			Harmon's Creek →
Woodland	Burial Mound II	300 B.C.		Hopewell	
Woodland	Burial Mound I	1000 B.C.		Adena	
Archaic	Archaic	2000 B.C.			
Archaic	Archaic	5000 B.C.	Indian Knoll		
Archaic		8000 B.C.			

Index